Collins

DINOSAURS

FASCINATING FACTS

Published by Collins
An imprint of HarperCollins Publishers
Westerhill Road
Bishopbriggs
Glasgow G64 2QT
www.harpercollins.co.uk

First published 2013
Second edition 2016

The contents of this publication are believed correct at the time of printing. Nevertheless the publisher can accept no responsibility for errors or omissions, changes in the detail given or for any expense or loss thereby caused.

HarperCollins does not warrant that any website mentioned in this title will be provided uninterrupted, that any website will be error free, that defects will be corrected, or that the website or the server that makes it available are free of viruses or bugs. For full terms and conditions please refer to the site terms provided on the website.

A catalogue record for this book is available from the British Library

ISBN 978-0-00-816928-2

10 9 8 7 6 5 4 3 2 1

Printed in China by R R Donnelley APS Co Ltd.

Collins Bartholomew, the UK's leading independent geographical information supplier, can provide a digital, custom, and premium mapping service to a variety of markets.
For further information:
Tel: +44 (0)208 307 4515
e-mail: collinsbartholomew@harpercollins.co.uk
Visit our website at: www.collins.co.uk   www.collinsbartholomew.com

If you would like to comment on any aspect of this book, please contact us at the above address or online.
e-mail: collinsmaps@harpercollins.co.uk

MIX
Paper from
responsible sources
FSC™ C007454

FSC™ is a non-profit international organisation established to promote the responsible management of the world's forests. Products carrying the FSC label are independently certified to assure consumers that they come from forests that are managed to meet the social, economic and ecological needs of present and future generations, and other controlled sources.

Find out more about HarperCollins and the environment at
www.harpercollins.co.uk/green

Contents

What is a Dinosaur?   4

Origins   6

Plant-eating Dinosaurs   8

Meat-eating Dinosaurs   9

Armoured Dinosaurs   10

Horned Dinosaurs   11

Body Shapes   12

Triassic   14

Jurassic   22

Cretaceous   38

Dinosaur Destruction   52

Dinosaur Remains   54

Dinosaur Anatomy   66

Activity   68

Index   70

What is a Dinosaur?

Millions of years ago before there were people there were dinosaurs. Dinosaurs were one group of prehistoric reptiles that dominated the land for over 160 million years.

They evolved in all shapes and sizes. Some were over 30 metres long and 15 metres tall, but others were only the size of a chicken. Some were meat-eaters and some plant-eaters. Some had thick, bumpy skin and some had primitive feathers. Some were armour-plated and some had horns or spikes.

All dinosaurs had straight legs and this allowed them to move much faster than many other reptiles. Dinosaurs could not fly and none lived in water.

Origins

The Age of Dinosaurs began 230 million years ago in the Triassic period when the world's landmass was one gigantic continent.

The first dinosaurs were small plant eaters and they roamed freely in all parts of the landmass. By the Jurassic period (208 – 144 million years ago) the landmass was breaking up into continents and climates everywhere were mild or warm. Some dinosaurs were now enormous and many were meat eaters. The first known bird, Archaeopteryx, appeared during this period.

During the Cretaceous period (144 – 65 million years ago) the landmasses were separated by seas and a huge variety of dinosaurs evolved, including the largest land predators ever. At the end of the Cretaceous period all dinosaurs died out.

50 million years ago

North America

Eurasia

South America

Africa

Antarctica

Australia

Laurasia

Laurasia

Gondwanaland

100 million years ago

Pangaea

Tethys

200 million years ago

150 million years ago

The Age of Dinosaurs - 230 to 65 million years ago

MESOZOIC ERA

200 MILLION YEARS AGO

251 MILLION YEARS

TRIASSIC PERIOD   JURASSIC   PERIOD   CRETACEOUS   PERIOD   TERTIARY

65 MILLION YEARS AGO   Palaeocene Epoch

CAMBRIAN PERIOD   ORDOVICIAN PERIOD   SILURIAN PERIOD

PALEOZOIC ERA

Eocene Epoch

PERMIAN   PERIOD

PENNSYLVANIAN   PERIOD   MISSISSIPPIAN PERIOD   DEVONIAN   PERIOD

PRECAMBRIAN

CENOZOIC ERA

Oligocene Epoch

11,500 YR.

1 BILLION YEARS AGO

Miocene Epoch   PERIOD

2 BILLION YEARS AGO

Pliocene Epoch   TERTIARY

3 BILLION YEARS AGO EARLIEST ORGANIC STRUCTURES

Holocene Epoch   Pleistocene Epoch   TERTIARY   PERIOD

4.5 BILLION YEARS AGO

QUATERNARY   PERIOD

Plant-eating Dinosaurs

Plant-eating dinosaurs are known as herbivores.

Plants grew throughout most of the Mesozoic era when dinosaurs were living. The plants were often poor in nutrients and difficult to digest and dinosaurs had to adapt to deal with this. Some needed to eat huge volumes of food to take in enough vitamins, while others used grinding teeth to break down the food before swallowing it.

Herbivores had long digestive systems to allow plants time to be properly broken down.

Brachiosaurus was a herbivore, but its teeth were not very good for grinding plants. Its stomach, however, contained stones (gastroliths) that did the grinding work.

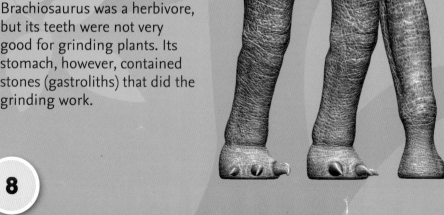

Meat-eating Dinosaurs

Meat-eating dinosaurs are known as carnivores.

These dinosaurs had huge jaws with front teeth designed to take great chunks out of their prey. They could slice through meat and tiny serrations in their teeth made it easy to cut through tough flesh.

Meat is easily digested so carnivores had quite short digestive systems.

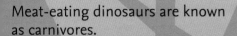

Tyrannosaurus was a carnivore. Its jaws were up to a metre long and had 60 teeth and a very powerful bite. Tyrannosaurus could eat up to 230 kg of meat and bones in one bite!

Armoured Dinosaurs

With savage predators such as the Allosaurus and Tyrannosaurus roaming the earth, some dinosaurs evolved to protect themselves from harm. Over time, they developed defensive features including strong body armour, spikes, plates and tough clubs on their tails to ward off any hungry carnivores.

The Ankylosaurus, shown below, is a well-known armoured dinosaur. To carry the weight of all this heavy armour this plant-eating dinosaur had very short, stout legs. By the time the Cretaceous period ended the Ankylosaurus was one of the few surviving dinosaurs thanks to its protective armour.

Horned Dinosaurs

Horned dinosaurs, such as the Triceratops shown below, are amongst the most recognisable dinosaurs. Most were herbivores with four legs and had huge heads, which displayed frills and pointed horns. It is not known if the frills were for protection, display or temperature control. Horned dinosaurs originated in Asia. They mainly inhabited North America but also lived in Europe.

Body Shapes

Sauropods

- Four-legged
- Long neck
- Long tail
- Small head
- Thick, pillar-like legs
- Very large

Ceratopians

- Four-legged
- Horned and frilled
- Beak
- Shearing teeth
- Medium-sized

Euornithopods

- Three-toed
- Curved spine
- Run on hind legs
- Horny beak
- No armour
- Stiff tail
- Medium-sized

Large Theropods

- Two-legged
- Clawed fingers
- Large jaws
- Small, bumpy scales
- Short front legs
- Large

Small Theropods

- Two-legged
- Clawed fingers
- Sometimes feathered
- Small and agile
- Bird-like body

Ankylosaurids

- Four-legged
- Heavy armour
- Clubbed tail
- Toothless beak
- Spikes
- Medium-sized

Ornithomimosaurs

- Ostrich-shaped
- Small head
- Large eyes
- Long, thin neck
- Strong toes with hoof-like claws
- Feathered

Triassic

The environment of the Triassic period was warm. Polar ice caps did not exist and the difference in temperature between the poles and the equator was much less than it is today. The continents were one landmass, with a desert environment in the centre. This made it difficult for life to exist in the centre of the continent, and most dinosaurs lived near the coasts.

Dinosaurs evolved in the Late Triassic along with crocodilians, pterosaurs (flying reptiles), and sea-reptiles. Some of the earliest discovered dinosaurs were two-legged hunters. Numerous Triassic dinosaur fossils have been found in South Africa, which was one of the most fertile areas during the Triassic period.

Plateosaurus

Say: plat-ee-oh-sore-us

Massive hind legs supported its body

Shorter front legs aided in walking and eating

Five-fingered hands and a large thumb claw

Fact file

My name means flat lizard
My length was 7 m
My height was 2 m – 3 m
My weight was 4000 kg
Teeth grinding teeth with a horny beak at the front
My diet was herbivorous

I ate plant material
How I moved on 2 or 4 legs
I lived in the Late Triassic (210 million years ago)
My home was Germany, France, Switzerland

Riojasaurus

Say: ree-oh-hah-sore-us

Heavy body

Long tail

Long neck to reach high-growing plants

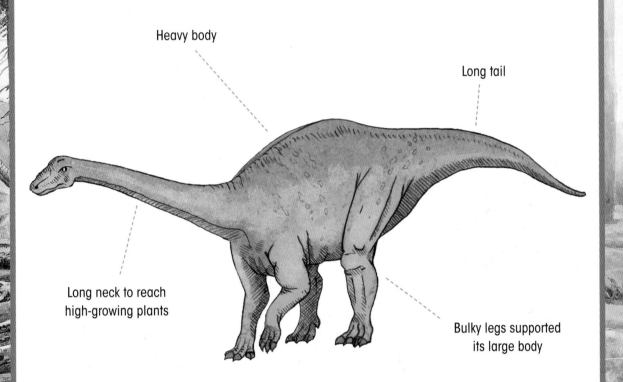

Bulky legs supported its large body

Fact file

My name means Rioja lizard
My length was 5.15 m
My height was 3 m
My weight was 1000 kg
Teeth leaf-shaped and serrated
My diet was herbivorous

I ate plant material especially high-growing plants
How I moved on 4 legs
I lived in the Late Triassic (221 – 210 million years ago)
My home was Argentina

Coelophysis

Say: seel-oh-fie-sis

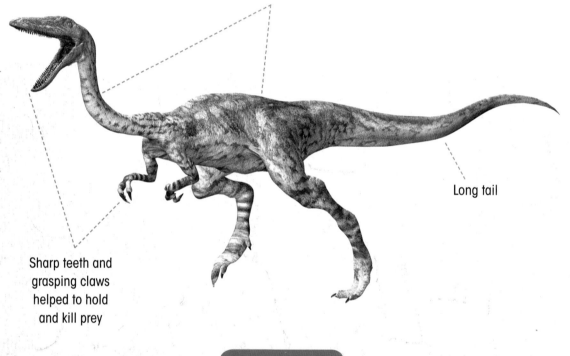

Light-weight body and long neck made it an excellent hunter. It was a quick and agile creature

Long tail

Sharp teeth and grasping claws helped to hold and kill prey

Fact file

My name means hollow form
My length was 3 m
My height was 2 m
My weight was 27 kg
Teeth small and sharp
My diet was carnivorous

I ate small reptiles and insects
How I moved on 2 legs
I lived in the Late Triassic
(225 – 220 million years ago)
My home was USA

Melanorosaurus

Say: me-lan-or-oh-sore-us

Long neck to eat high-growing vegetation

Bulky body

Elephant-like legs

Long tail

Fact file

My name means Black Mountain lizard
My length was 12 m
My height was 4 m
My weight was 1000 kg
Teeth serrated and leaf-shaped
My diet was herbivorous

I ate leaves from trees
How I moved on 4 legs
I lived in the Late Triassic
(227 – 221 million years ago)
My home was South Africa

Staurikosaurus

Say: stor-ik-oh-sore-us

Teeth were serrated and curved backwards to aid eating

Long tail, compared to the rest of its body, helped it to leap and run

Powerful hind legs made it a fast runner

Fact file

My name means Southern Cross lizard
My length was 2 m
My height was 0.8 m
My weight was 30 kg
Teeth curved backwards and serrated
My diet was carnivorous

I ate small animals
How I moved on 2 legs
I lived in the Late Triassic (227 – 221 million years ago)
My home was Brazil

Mussaurus

Say: moos-sore-us

Tall skull, short snout
and large eyes

Long neck

Long tail

Fact file

My **name means** mouse lizard
My **length was** 3 m
My **height was** 1 m
My **weight was** 70 kg
Teeth sharp, leaf-shaped
My **diet was** herbivorous

I ate plant material
How I moved on 2 or 4 legs
I lived in the Late Triassic
(221 – 210 million years ago)
My home was Argentina

Jurassic

During the Jurassic period two major continents, Laurasia and Gondwana, were formed. Underwater volcanic activity caused the ocean floor to spread and water levels to rise. Oceans were small and shallow and the climate was warm and tropical. Many large, dense forests began to appear. Some of the most common plants were large conifers and thick ferns.

Dinosaurs evolved to be gigantic. Many titanic sauropods became common including Brachiosaurus. These were pursued by large predators like the Ceratosaurus and the well-known Allosaurus. These large dinosaurs may have influenced the evolution of the first armoured dinosaurs like the Stegosaurus.

Lesothosaurus

Say: Le-so-toe-sore-us

Pointed teeth with grooved edges for chewing through plants

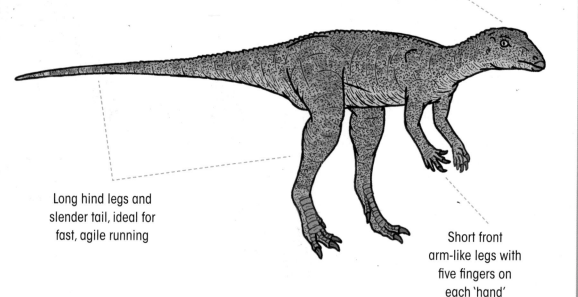

Long hind legs and slender tail, ideal for fast, agile running

Short front arm-like legs with five fingers on each 'hand'

Fact file

My name means Lesotho lizard
My length was 1 m
My height was 0.5 m
My weight was 10 kg
Teeth small grinding teeth
My diet was herbivorous

I ate plant material
How I moved on 2 legs
I lived in the Early Jurassic
(213 – 200 million years ago)
My home was Lesotho, South Africa

Cryolophosaurus

Say: cry-o-loaf-oh-sore-us

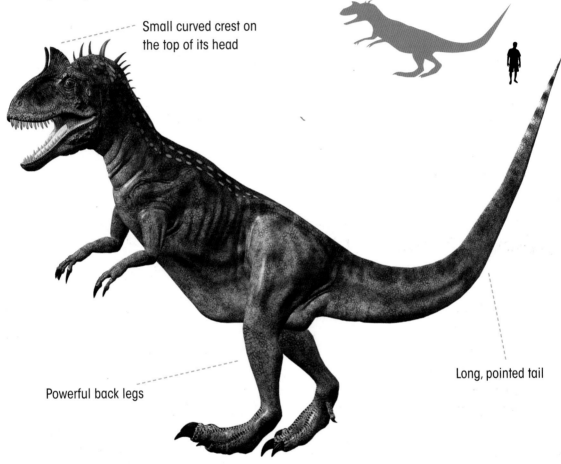

Small curved crest on the top of its head

Powerful back legs

Long, pointed tail

Fact file

My **name means** frozen crested lizard
My **length was** 8 m
My **height was** 3 m
My **weight was** 500 kg
Teeth many sharp and pointed teeth
My **diet was** carnivorous

I ate other animals
How I moved on 2 legs
I lived in the Early Jurassic (170 million years ago)
My home was Antarctica

Dilophosaurus

Say: die-loaf-oh-sore-us

Pair of thin, bony crests
on its head may have
been for display

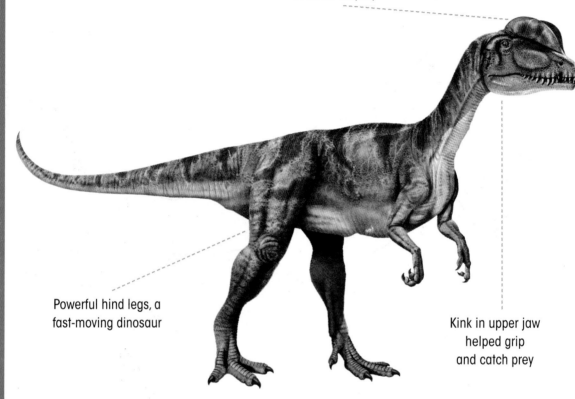

Powerful hind legs, a
fast-moving dinosaur

Kink in upper jaw
helped grip
and catch prey

Fact file

My **name means** double-crested lizard
My **length was** 6 m
My **height was** 2 m
My **weight was** 300 kg – 450 kg
Teeth lots of sharp and curved teeth
My **diet was** carnivorous

I ate other animals
How I moved on 2 legs
I lived in the Early Jurassic
(190 million years ago)
My home was USA

Megalosaurus

Say: meg-ah-low-sore-us

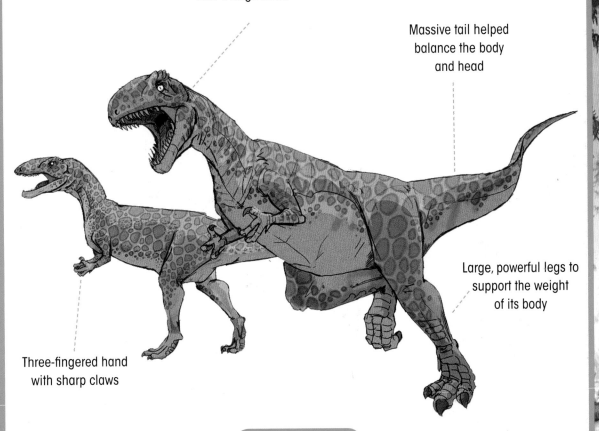

Strong, short neck with a large head

Massive tail helped balance the body and head

Three-fingered hand with sharp claws

Large, powerful legs to support the weight of its body

Fact file

My **name means** great lizard
My **length was** 9 m
My **height was** 3 m
My **weight was** 1000 kg
Teeth sharp and serrated
My **diet was** carnivorous

I ate other large animals
How I moved on 2 legs
I lived in the Mid Jurassic
(170 – 155 million years ago)
My home was France, United Kingdom

Archaeopteryx

Say: ark-ee-opt-er-ix

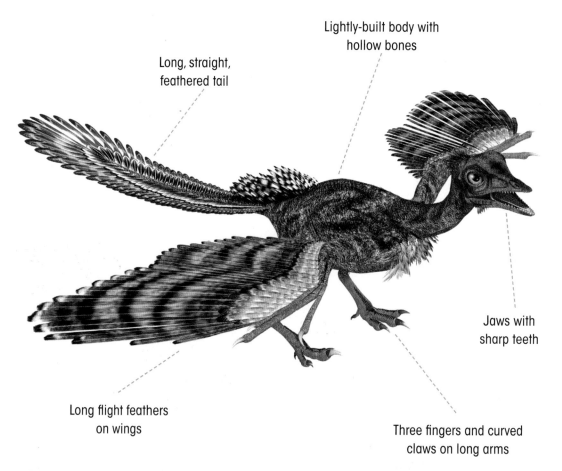

Lightly-built body with hollow bones

Long, straight, feathered tail

Jaws with sharp teeth

Long flight feathers on wings

Three fingers and curved claws on long arms

Fact file

My name means ancient wing
My length was 0.5 m
My height was 0.2 m
My weight was 0.4 kg – 0.5 kg
Teeth many small conical teeth in the upper jaw

My diet was carnivorous
I ate small reptiles, mammals or insects
How I moved on 2 legs and by flying
I lived in the Late Jurassic (147 million years ago)
My home was Germany

Compsognathus

Say: komp-sog-nath-us

Long tail used for balance
when moving

Hollow bones
made it very light

Long pointed head
with sharp teeth

Long, slender legs and
elongated feet made it
fast and agile

Fact file

My **name means** pretty jaw
My **length was** 0.65 m
My **height was** 0.7 m
My **weight was** 3.6 kg
Teeth small and sharp
My **diet was** carnivorous

I **ate** small animals and insects
How I moved on 2 legs
I lived in the Late Jurassic
(145 – 140 million years ago)
My home was Germany, France

Stegosaurus

Say: steg-oh-sore-us

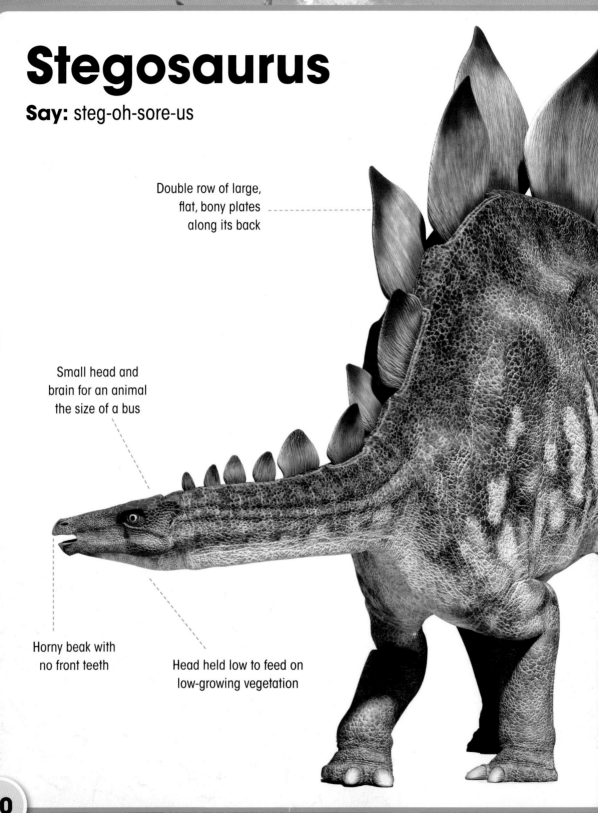

Double row of large, flat, bony plates along its back

Small head and brain for an animal the size of a bus

Horny beak with no front teeth

Head held low to feed on low-growing vegetation

Powerful spiked tail
for protection

Back legs twice as
long as front legs

Fact file

My name means roof lizard
My length was 9 m
My height was 4 m
My weight was 5000 kg
Teeth small, triangular and flat
My diet was herbivorous
I ate plant material
How I moved on 4 legs
I lived in the Late Jurassic
(156 – 144 million years ago)
My home was USA

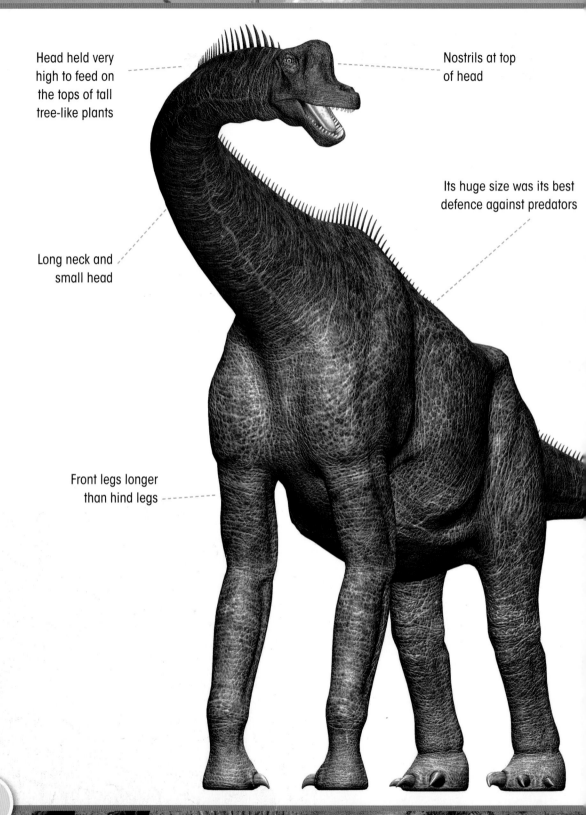

Head held very
high to feed on
the tops of tall
tree-like plants

Nostrils at top
of head

Its huge size was its best
defence against predators

Long neck and
small head

Front legs longer
than hind legs

Brachiosaurus

Say: brak-ee-oh-sore-us

Long, thick tail which could be used to repel attackers

Fact file

My name means arm lizard
My length was 30 m
My height was 12 – 16 m
My weight was 30 000 kg – 80 000 kg
Teeth chisel-shaped
My diet was herbivorous
I ate leaves from trees
How I moved on 4 legs
I lived in the Late Jurassic
(155 – 140 million years ago)
My home was Tanzania, USA, Portugal, Algeria

Kentrosaurus

Say: ken-troh-sore-us

Spiky, flexible tail made it a dangerous weapon

Double row of bony plates and spikes running down its back and tail

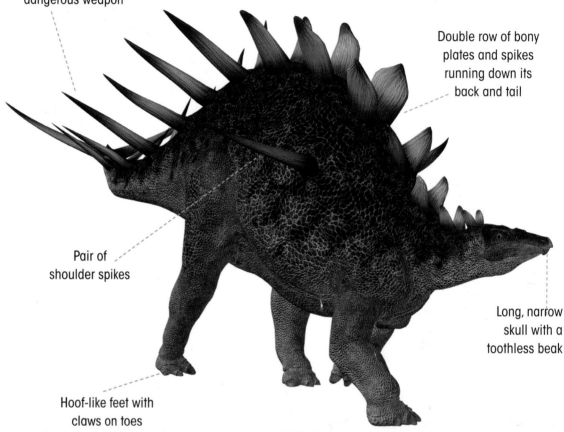

Pair of shoulder spikes

Long, narrow skull with a toothless beak

Hoof-like feet with claws on toes

Fact file

My name means spiky lizard
My length was 5 m
My height was 1.8 m
My weight was 2000 kg
Teeth toothless beak and small cheek teeth

My diet was herbivorous
I ate plant material
How I moved on 4 legs
I lived in the Late Jurassic (155 – 150 million years ago)
My home was Tanzania

Diplodocus

Say: di-plod-oh-kuss

Long, whip-like tail which counter balanced the long neck

Small head and brain

Long neck used to reach vegetation and drinking water

Large gut, needed to digest lots of plant material

Fact file

My name means double beam
My length was 26 m
My height was 8 m
My weight was 20 000 kg – 25 000 kg
Teeth rows of teeth like a comb
My diet was herbivorous

I ate leaves from trees and soft plants
How I moved on 4 legs
I lived in the Late Jurassic
(155 – 145 million years ago)
My home was USA

Allosaurus

Say: al-oh-saw-russ

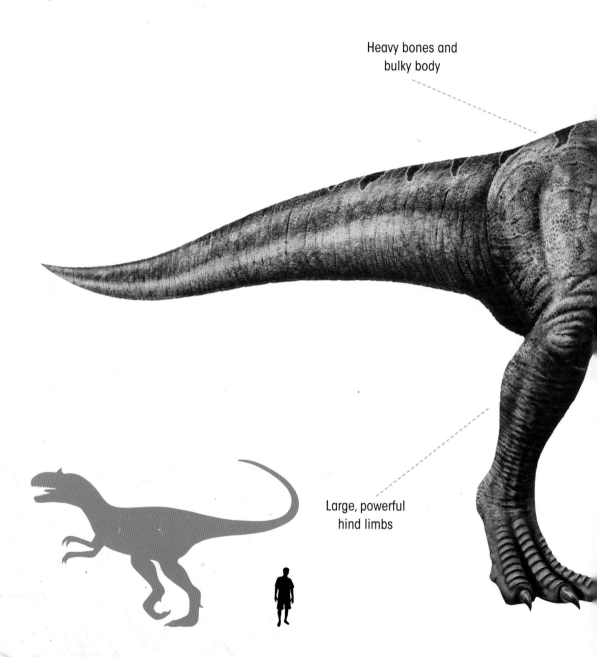

Heavy bones and
bulky body

Large, powerful
hind limbs

Bony knobs and ridges on top of head

Teeth 5 – 10 cm long and curved backwards to prevent prey from escaping

Fact file

My name means other lizard
My length was 12 m
My height was 5 m
My weight was 2000 kg
Teeth dagger-like with serrated edges
My diet was carnivorous
I ate large plant eating dinosaurs
How I moved on 2 legs
I lived in the Late Jurassic
(153 – 135 million years ago)
My home was Tanzania, USA

Cretaceous

At the beginning of the Cretaceous period the climate was warm and humid. Flowering plants began to appear for the first time. This led to an increase in insect populations. Landmasses separated into the continents as we know them today.

The Cretaceous period saw the appearance of more dinosaurs than ever before. The horned Cretaceous dinosaurs appeared, like the Triceratops and Centrosaurus. The armoured Ankylosaurus and large carnivore Tyrannosaurus were two of the quickly evolving dinosaurs.

Hypsilophodon

Say: hip-sih-loh-foh-don

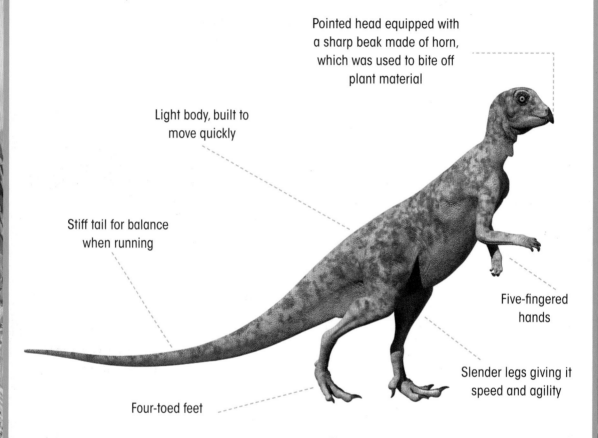

Pointed head equipped with a sharp beak made of horn, which was used to bite off plant material

Light body, built to move quickly

Stiff tail for balance when running

Five-fingered hands

Slender legs giving it speed and agility

Four-toed feet

Fact file

My name means high-ridge tooth
My length was 2.3 m
My height was 0.8 m
My weight was 50 kg
Teeth horny beak and self-sharpening cheek teeth
My diet was herbivorous

I ate plant material
How I moved on 2 legs
I lived in the Early Cretaceous (125 million years ago)
My home was United Kingdom, Spain

Baryonyx

Say: bah-ree-on-icks

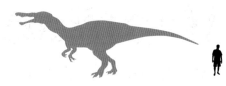

Long, low snout with narrow jaws like a crocodile

Sturdy rear legs supported its low-slung body

Long claws on its thumbs, used to catch fish

Fact file

My name means heavy claw
My length was 10 m
My height was 4 m
My weight was 2000 kg
Teeth sharp, finely serrated
My diet was carnivorous

I ate fish, Iguanodon
How I moved on 2 legs
I lived in the Early Cretaceous
(125 million years ago)
My home was United Kingdom,
Spain, Portugal

Iguanodon

Say: ig-wha-noh-don

Large thumb spikes, probably for defense against predators

Long tongue

Backbone and tail stiffened by tendons

Flexible little finger which aided food gathering

Powerful legs but not built for running

Fact file

My **name means** iguana tooth
My **length was** 10 m
My **height was** 3 – 5 m
My **weight was** 4000 kg – 5000 kg
Teeth chewing cheek teeth and horny beak
My **diet was** herbivorous

I **ate** plant material
How I moved on 2 or 4 legs
I **lived in the** Early Cretaceous (140 – 110 million years ago)
My **home was** United Kingdom, Germany, USA, Spain, Belgium

Psittacosaurus

Say: sit-ak-oh-sore-us

Powerful beak on the upper jaw

Long, quill-like structures on its tail and lower back, possibly used for display

Skull was tall in height and short in length

Fact file

My name means parrot lizard
My length was 2 m
My height was 1 m
My weight was 50 kg
Teeth beak
My diet was herbivorous

I ate plant material
How I moved on 2 or 4 legs
I lived in the Early Cretaceous (120 – 100 million years ago)
My home was China, Mongolia, Russia, Thailand

Tyrannosaurus

Say: tie-ran-oh-sore-us

Stiff, heavy tail used
to counterbalance its
enormous head

Large, powerful
hind legs

Sixty teeth, each one up to 20 cm long. Its bite was around three times as powerful as that of a great white shark

Massive skull with powerful jaw

Small but unusually powerful arms with two clawed fingers

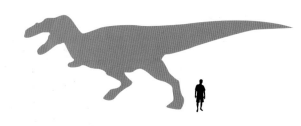

Fact file

My name means tyrant lizard
My length was 12 m
My height was 5.6 m
My weight was 7000 kg
Teeth 60 saw-edged, bone-crushing, pointed teeth

My diet was carnivorous
I ate other animals
How I moved on 2 legs
I lived in the Late Cretaceous (67 – 65 million years ago)
My home was Canada, USA

Triceratops

Say: tri-serra-tops

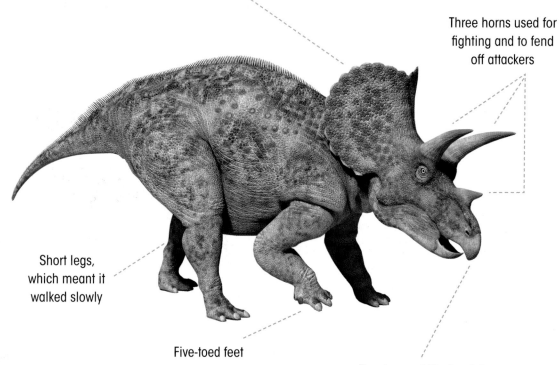

Large frill, up to 1 metre across, which helped to protect its neck

Three horns used for fighting and to fend off attackers

Short legs, which meant it walked slowly

Five-toed feet

Tough parrot-like beak for plucking low-growing plants

Fact file

My name means three-horned face
My length was 9 m
My height was 3 m
My weight was 5500 kg
Teeth horny beak and shearing teeth
My diet was herbivorous

I ate tough palm fronds
How I moved on 4 legs
I lived in the Late Cretaceous
(67 – 65 million years ago)
My home was Canada, USA

Euoplocephalus

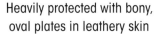

Say: you-oh-plo-kef-ah-luss

Heavily protected with bony, oval plates in leathery skin

Bony club tail used to defend it from predators

Rows of bony spikes along its body

Short, drooping snout with horny beak

Large gut needed to digest huge amounts of plant material

Short, sturdy legs

Fact file

My name means well-armoured head
My length was 7 m
My height was 1.8 m
My weight was 2000 kg
Teeth horny beak and cheek teeth
My diet was herbivorous

I ate plant material
How I moved on 4 legs
I lived in the Late Cretaceous (76 – 70 million years ago)
My home was Canada, USA

Ankylosaurus

Say: an-kie-loh-sore-us

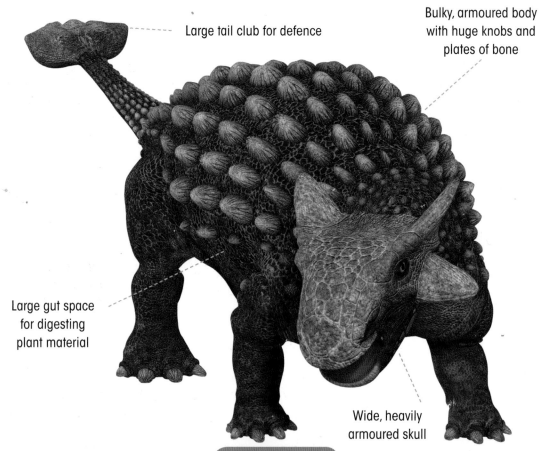

Large tail club for defence

Bulky, armoured body with huge knobs and plates of bone

Large gut space for digesting plant material

Wide, heavily armoured skull

Fact file

My name means stiff lizard
My length was 7 m
My height was 2.5 m
My weight was 4000 kg – 7000 kg
Teeth small, leaf-shaped teeth with a horny beak at the front

My diet was herbivorous
I ate plant material
How I moved on 4 legs
I lived in the Late Cretaceous (74 – 67 million years ago)
My home was Canada, USA

Spinosaurus

Say: spine-oh-sore-us

Tall spines, up to 1.8 metres long, forming a sail-like fin which may have helped to regulate its temperature

Flexible upper spine so it could arch its back

Long, narrow skull, similar to a crocodile, with powerful jaws

Muscular legs for running quickly

Fact file

My name means thorn lizard
My length was 18 m
My height was 5 m
My weight was 4000 kg
Teeth flat and blade-like with no serrations

My diet was carnivorous
I ate fish and other dinosaurs
How I moved on 2 legs
I lived in the Late Cretaceous (95 – 70 million years ago)
My home was Egypt, Morocco

49

Velociraptor

Say: vel-oss-ee-rap-tor

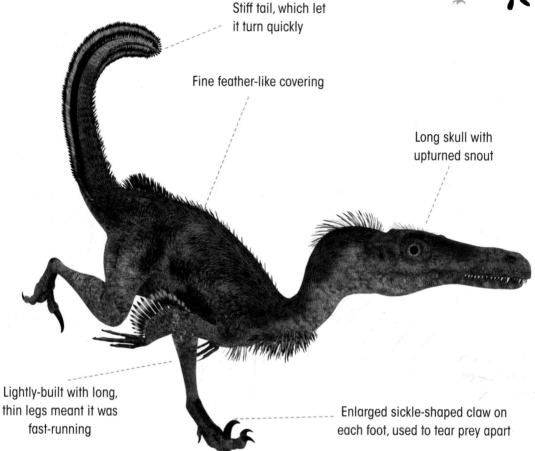

Stiff tail, which let it turn quickly

Fine feather-like covering

Long skull with upturned snout

Lightly-built with long, thin legs meant it was fast-running

Enlarged sickle-shaped claw on each foot, used to tear prey apart

Fact file

My name means quick plunderer
My length was 1.8 m
My height was 1 m
My weight was 7 kg – 15 kg
Teeth lots of sharp, pointed teeth
My diet was carnivorous

I ate other animals
How I moved on 2 legs
I lived in the Late Cretaceous (84 – 80 million years ago)
My home was Mongolia, China

Parasaurolophus

Say: pa-ra-saw-rol-off-us

Long, hollow, bony crest up to
1.8 metres long, which may have
made a sound like a foghorn

Powerful hind legs

Spoon-shaped beak
used to browse on
plant material

Fact file

My name means like 'Saurolophus'
My length was 11 m
My height was 5.2 m
My weight was 3500 kg
Teeth beak and toothed jaws
My diet was herbivorous

I ate pine needles, tree leaves, twigs
How I moved on 2 or 4 legs
I lived in the Late Cretaceous
(76 – 74 million years ago)
My home was Canada, USA

Dinosaur Destruction

Dinosaurs became extinct about 65 million years ago at the end of the Cretaceous period. About 70 per cent of all animal life on earth died out at that time. Scientists call it a mass extinction. This suggests that a catastrophic event took place at that time causing unfavourable changes in the environment to which the dinosaurs could not adapt.

There are many different theories about what happened but we will probably never know the exact details.

Some popular theories include asteroid impact, an ice age, volcanic activity, widespread disease or competition from other animals. Maybe a combination of all these factors was responsible for their death.

Dinosaur extinction remains a big mystery. Although dinosaurs died out at this time, many species survived, including similar animal types like crocodiles.

Dinosaur Remains
North America

North America has a rich dinosaur fossil record with a great variety of dinosaurs. The first discovery of dinosaur remains in North America was made in 1854 when a small collection of isolated teeth were found near the upper Missouri River. The first complete skeletons were found in the late 1870s in Colorado and Wyoming.

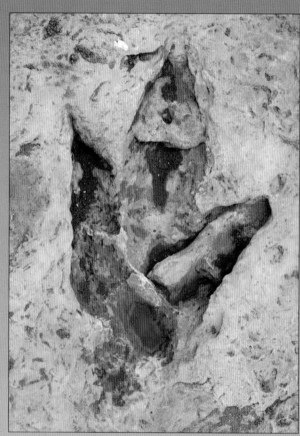

Dinosaur footprint near Tulsa, USA

Fossil map

- Fossil locations

NORTH
AMERICA

Dinosaur Remains
South America

As far as palaeontologists (people who study fossils) can tell, the very first dinosaurs originated in South America. While South American dinosaurs weren't quite as diverse as those on other continents, many of them were noteworthy in their own right.

Fossils of the Guaibasaurus, like this one, can be found in Brazil

Fossil map

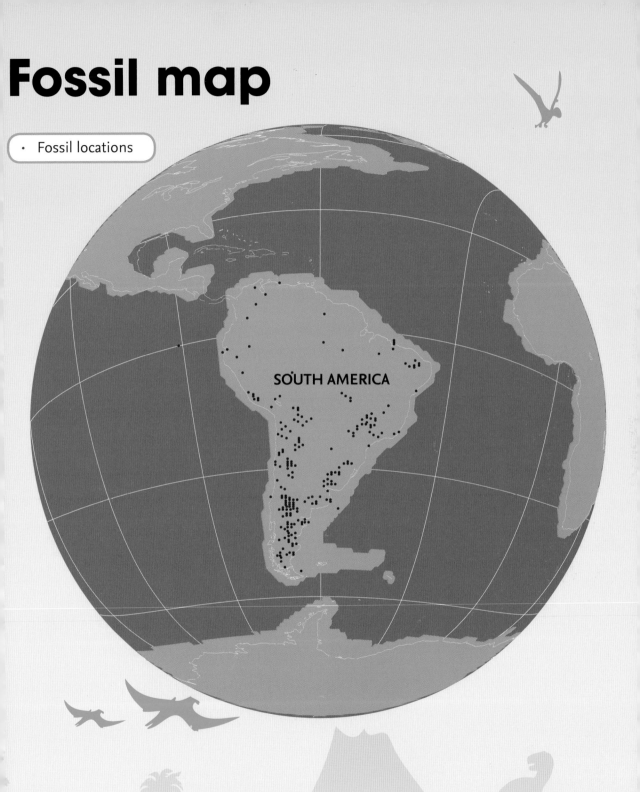

· Fossil locations

SOUTH AMERICA

Dinosaur Remains
Europe

Much of what is known about European dinosaurs dates from the period around the Jurassic-Cretaceous boundary. There is a rich record of fossils from this period. Fewer fossils have been discovered from the rest of the age when dinosaurs inhabited the planet.

A theropod fossil from Peinten, Germany

Fossil map

EUROPE

59

Dinosaur Remains
Africa

The species of dinosaurs that lived in Africa were among the fiercest on the planet. Fossil records are patchy and incomplete although the Triassic and Early Jurassic periods are well represented. The Early Cretaceous was an important time for the dinosaurs of Africa because this was when Africa finally separated from South America, forming the South Atlantic Ocean. It was an important event because the dinosaurs became isolated and developed unique characteristics as they adapted to specific environments.

Dinosaur footprints in the Namibian desert

Fossil map

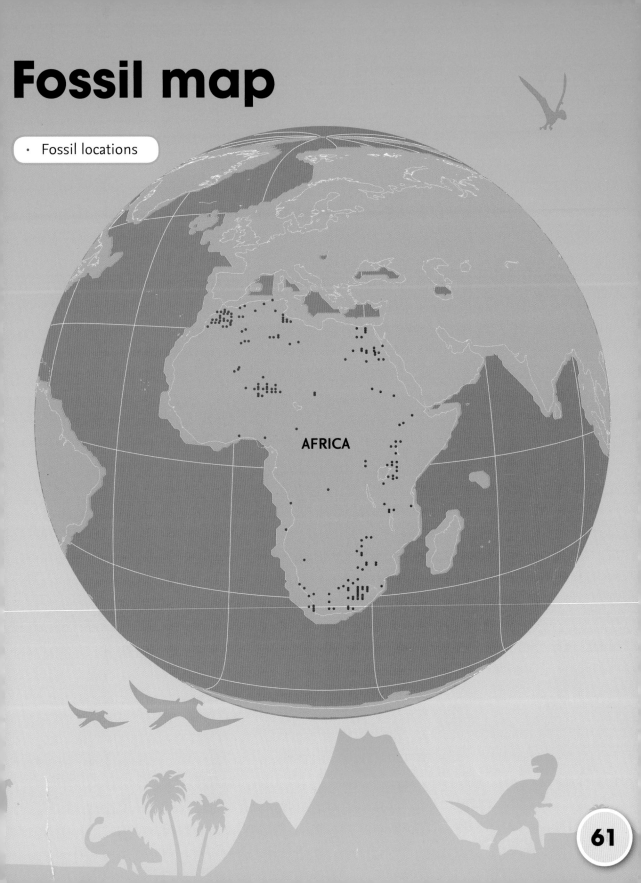

· Fossil locations

AFRICA

Dinosaur Remains
Asia

Over the past few decades, more dinosaurs have been discovered in central and eastern Asia than on any other continent. India was separated from Asia during the time of the dinosaurs. However, it was connected to Madagascar throughout much of the dinosaur era and they shared similar dinosaur species, distinct from what has been found on the modern-day African and Asian landmasses.

Dinosaur fossil in rock and sand in Yunnan, China

Fossil map

ASIA

Dinosaur Remains
Australasia and Antarctica

Australia and Antarctica hosted their fair share of theropods, sauropods and ornithopods, however, in comparison to the rest of the world, finds of dinosaur fossils have been insignificant. This is partly because

Australia was covered by a shallow sea for most of the dinosaur era and since then there has been very little movement of mountains – an event that would normally expose fossils.

A restored theropod skull at the Australian Museum, Sydney

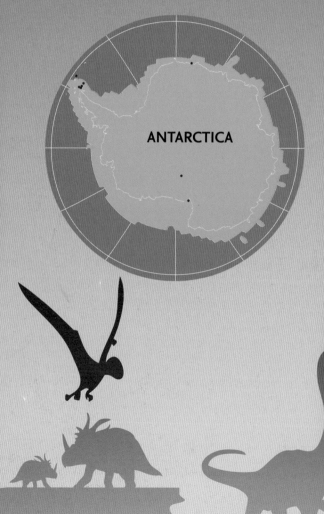

ANTARCTICA

Fossil map

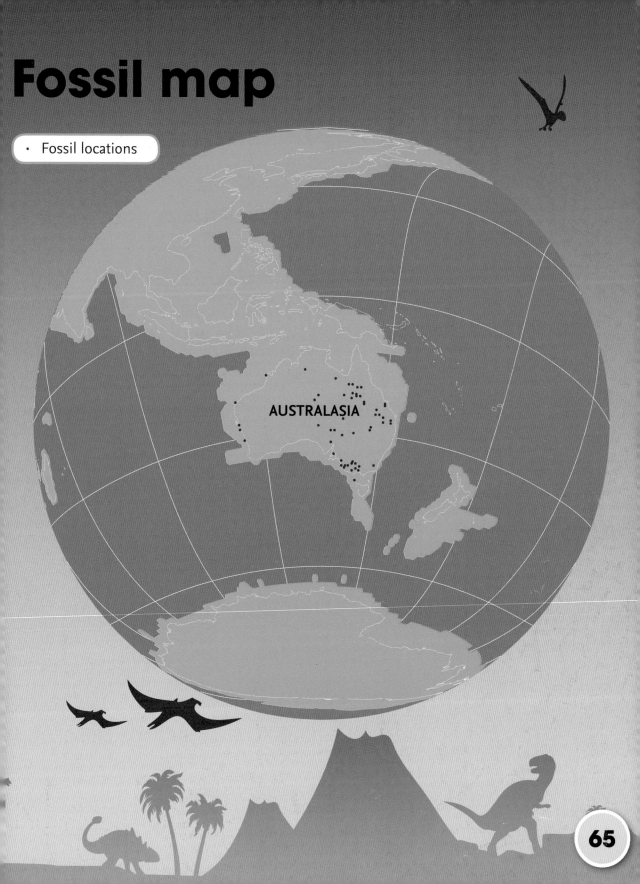

- Fossil locations

AUSTRALASIA

Dinosaur Anatomy

A dinosaur's body was designed and worked in much the same way as any other land animal with a backbone.

A dinosaur's bony skeleton supported muscles for movement and protected its internal organs such as its brain, heart and lungs. The big, heavy dinosaurs had solid bones and the lighter ones had hollow bones. A dinosaur's muscles helped to hold all the bones together, gave it a characteristic shape and made it move.

The digestive system was made up of a long gut with lots of overlapping coils or folds. The gut of carnivores was less complicated than that of herbivores as flesh was easier to digest than plant material.

Dinosaurs' hearts pumped blood around their bodies and their lungs breathed in air containing oxygen. Many dinosaurs stood tall and walked liked elephants and ostriches and this makes scientists think that they all had big hearts like mammals and birds.

Like any animal a dinosaur also had a nervous system to control its body. The control centre was its brain, which was well developed to guide movement, sight and smell. The thinking part of its brain was very small. The most intelligent dinosaurs were no brainier than birds.

Vertebra

Intestines

Lungs

Ribs

Scapula

Vertebra

Heart

Stomach

Activity

Dinosaurs came in all shapes, sizes and colours. Colour these popular dinosaurs.

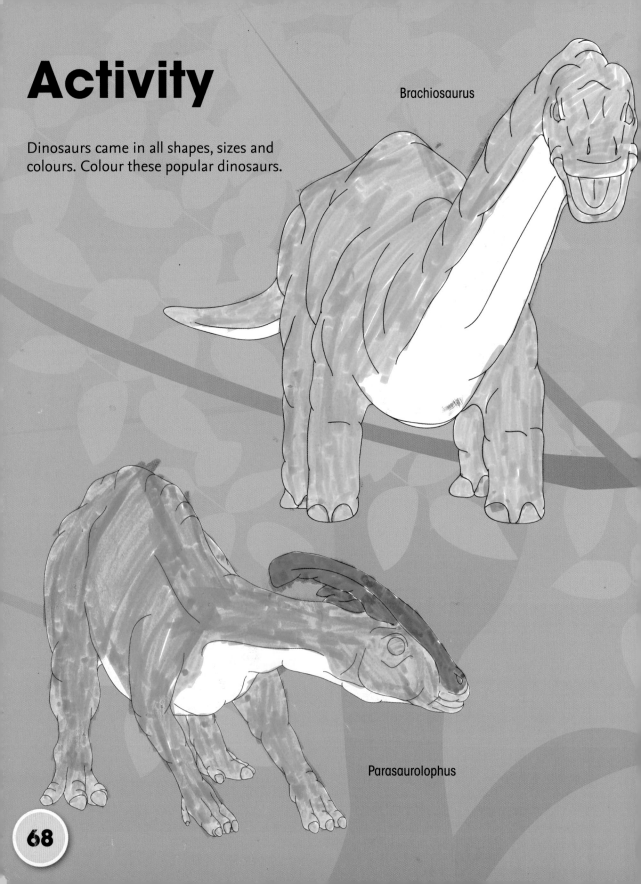

Brachiosaurus

Parasaurolophus

Triceratops

Tyrannosaurus

69